# Vestiges

*poems by*

# Jacob Minasian

*Finishing Line Press*
Georgetown, Kentucky

# Vestiges

Copyright © 2023 by Jacob Minasian
ISBN 979-8-88838-087-1 First Edition
All rights reserved under International and Pan-American Copyright Conventions.
No part of this book may be reproduced in any manner whatsoever without written permission from the publisher, except in the case of brief quotations embodied in critical articles and reviews.

## ACKNOWLEDGMENTS

Lines from "Early Fall" were first published as "Canopy" in Sledgehammer Literary Journal.

Thank you to Nicholas Cuzzi and Matthew Zapruder for their generosity and encouragement during the making of this book.

And my deepest gratitude to my family. This book would not exist without you.

Publisher: Leah Huete de Maines
Editor: Christen Kincaid
Cover Art: Jacob Minasian
Author Photo: Helena Minasian
Cover Design: Elizabeth Maines McCleavy

Order online: www.finishinglinepress.com
also available on amazon.com

Author inquiries and mail orders:
Finishing Line Press
P. O. Box 1626
Georgetown, Kentucky 40324
U. S. A.

# Table of Contents

Winter ................................................................. 1

Late Winter ...................................................... 11

Haiku ................................................................ 17

Spring ............................................................... 23

Summer ........................................................... 29

Late Summer ................................................... 41

Early Fall .......................................................... 49

Crown .............................................................. 53

Fall .................................................................... 69

*For my wife,
and for my daughter*

Μνάσεσθαί τινα φαμί και ύστερον αμμέων
Someone will remember us after
—Sappho

# Winter

Listening to the weather
report, and hearing
wind wanting the windows,
or the woman who,
out in the night's
depth, in the
complex street, threatens
a man that she'll kill
herself, just before
she turns her car
into a bolt, I try to
settle myself between
expectations of work
and temperature,
all of the white outside.
I crack an antacid
anhydrous wafer
to fit through a water
bottle's neck near
frozen, hear
the slow dissolve in the cold
in my Camry, Interstate
275 through Cincinnati, speed
limited, breathing words at
vents reluctantly warming
the visible $CO_2$ at my teeth.
In the exterior blur
a salted metal
fender still
hangs from a side rail.
Yesterday, it all appeared
ski-lodge, resort, now
apocalyptic, all
beauty muted—roads
dimmed and ashen,
gravity pulling crisp
dunes into a blender.
Pools of ice meld
with the asphalt's ebony.

Everything is cancelled
except commerce as,
of course, according
to systemic mores,
the freeze frees more feet
for foot traffic braving
the degrees too
low for their own
dodged obligations.
And, as a day
passes, the freeze drops
lower. A parking
garage elevator
does not want to open,
the steel appealing
to its own tendency
toward resistance.
I muscle my tires
through ossifying
heaps, step out into
negative wind, measured
too dangerous to breathe
for too long, and statue
at the sight of two deer
running a clearing cleared
by the alarming oxygen,
one leaping to clear a set
of pebbled steps. The
strength and
grace inescapably
move mind to
mythology. Blood.
Hooves thudding like
arrows against flesh.

*Breath cuts
the wind with its
last jagged pulls.
Black open
eyes under
antlers. They
should not have
reached so deeply
into the density
of Artemis' charge,
these men controlled
by self-endowed
absolution. A quick
bronze-headed
arrow let go by
Agamemnon's order,
and now tongue
missiles the teeth,
the lungs churn
smoke out into air through
heaving nostrils, wet, drying,
the heart bleeding into grass
and soil, through ribs and muscle
and tendon, a hoof kicking
empty. Artemis draws this
moment into her own bow. She inhales,
weaves it to the wind, attaching
the black eyes and shuddering heart
and vanishing breath, stitches it
to the sails of the conquering
ships, the soldiers, their shoulders,
the galleys, their masts, the
plans and parchment charted
with bloated ambitions.
To the war itself.
So that it would all
stop together.
Agamemnon's army looks
out over the resting waves,*

*the vast ocean turning
to glass, the calming
current denying its path.*

Staring at the ocean
is what I used to
do on days
the water didn't feel
too far away, when
my hands peeled
pine curtains, pages
in perception's pocket.
Harbor seals tossed like
persons in the surf,
pelicans swinging
low as if posing
for pictures batteries
were too dead to take.
Between fingers, a
sand dollar is the size
of a rock face, covered
by barnacles, pocks filling
with anemones in
green-pink flares,
razor-tipped mussel
shell horizons hiding
below the swarming tide.
A sandal dodges its
heel in the cold wet step
I will never retrace.
Though this is California,
and my body's in Ohio,
2019, standing in contrast's
sharpening bite, amidst
snow and red ball caps
with white lettering.
The first of the
month arrives the
same as the end
of the last.
Groundsmen make
their rounds with salt
in orange buckets.

A new falling has
freshened the landscape,
the business-minded once
again emerging to worry
in public, sipping
seasonal mochas and
reading stocks off their
listening phones, news
from comment
streams on their feeds,
thinking car
payments while sending
digital balloons for a
sibling's injury. The
government is closed;
debates happen under heat
vents while workers
consider mortgages and
meal plans. A warm day
approaches on the forecast
and I pass a lake where
the previous spring a great
blue heron gusted its wing-
span into a landing on the
dark green mottled surface.
Beautiful, though to say
those were lighter times
would be like saying we had less
to worry about when we were
only drilling holes for oil.

*Athena sends the heron's
flight as herald,
Odysseus' eyes upward,
the crescent's light
caressing retinas.
Waves heave hull
with hypnotic undulations
under the sky's shimmering clarity.
The large gray bird, silent,
presents intention through presence,
the same way a bolt is
lightning, leaving, lockdown.
Time watches us.
Odysseus' ship slips alongside
the fleet, a cleaver
slicing toward the dark mirror's
thin hinge.*

Pivoting, I jot a haiku for the
other side of the argument:

> There's a certain panic
> that sets in, knowing
> there's no convincing.

In California, the burrowing owls
have been built over.
Atop long legs used to sprint
or shovel, the owls' heads swivel with
bright yellow sentinel stares, their gait
patient and ostrich quick. They warily
direct their attention,
feathered compasses,
ducking sideways like 1920's
gangsters in a bright light
over a barrel of moonshine,
their burrows just
outside the bay on a patchy grass
corner now bulldozed and
buried by human compartments.
Back in Cincinnati, the climate
warms to a rainstorm,
steam wafting from the plowed
roadside mounds off Waterstone.
I'm home and hit the television
remote against
my kneecap neurotically.
The silence of two a.m.
amplifies breath. There's
an argument through the walls.
The clock finds its awareness.
My fiancé sleeps
and I love her impossibly.

# Late Winter

How long I have
walked in parking
lots past people
set to fight
others over
a few feet less
to an entrance,
having visions of
planets completely
covered in bitumen,
white lines, and cars with
human heads breaking
over hoods like prairie
dogs. A customer returns
meat green from weeks
too long in the refrigerator
as a saxophone falsettos the
breath of a man on a street
in Philadelphia with
no walls to house his refrain.

Within the drive to
Pennsylvania, early
through Ohio, on a
sparse stretch
of highway, billboards
preach exclusion: a pair
of gold bands,
one gender combination
for marriage.
A Confederate flag is
painted large on a barn
roof, faded,
as if stretched to tear.
Native American
names are attributed
to every category of
noun without
proper homage.
The Appalachian
Mountains rise through
the left window right
before the tolls begin,
and a hawk, its
wingspan inducing
awe, dives to
grab roadside
trash in its talons—
a styrofoam cup now
crushed to confetti.

*Pearl feathers snow from
the hawk's scaled clutch,
down to Telemachus, his crew,
oars in fists, wood wedging Ithaca
grain. The dove
shows bright its own dismantling.
Theoclymenus, the seer, speaks
premonition to the prince, leveling
a rooted hand up at
Apollo's call.
Those who arrive at power
through belligerent appropriation
will find themselves excised.*

Tailpipes burn
like ugly cigars staring
back in traffic.
Water, frozen in the roads'
fractures, opens
divots that hit
tires like concussions.
Just as the light falls
away from the sky,
westbound, where the
275 rises past its industry
to a slight hover,
and the dimensional flare
of thousands of ordinary
utilities ignites a gemstone
array along the walls of a dark
curved spacial relation, I find
a fleeting meditation, which
sinks away with the asphalt,
and the tragedy of condition
quickly resettles.
An overlarge target on a gun
range sign
pushes buying instruments
to burn life, or, at least, to practice,
black targets on white paper.
I question whether
to lament, which
is the same as think
about my surroundings.
I arrive home, a shell in a sandstorm.

# Haiku

With context, a prayer
to die is ambiguous.
The snared state constructs

obvious knowledge
of opposite intention.
One can't contemplate

how near one always
is constantly to death, or
the wound opens to

the mark of scarring.
Un-grapple-able tragedy
stakes one's intestines.

The great holder, the
things one can't say or unsay,
the blinding shadow

contouring every
fragile facet and fabric
in a day's pathos.

Relief from regret
is a warm stew on the green
side of bulletproofed

glass. Absolution
is no absolute notion.
There is no direct

line between tears and
flawless bravado that isn't
a prism of mass

construction. People
and pollution, hand by hand,
the societal

blisters that boil up from
where we all least like to look,
or just one of the

many spots under stone
left purposefully unflipped.
Most don't remember

the night had when three
nights removed. Think about the
relevancy of

significance. Or
the significance of that
relevancy. In

Ohio the wine,
a pricey California-
grown pinot noir

bottle, gets placed at
the edge of the top of the
refrigerator,

with a single shake
able to topple it off,
by those who have not

felt the punch of a
fault line. Ground exponential.
The lime sizzles as

if roasting at the
top of my beer. Meaning eats
letters. Awareness

dines itself into
my synapses. To untie
or to unite is

decided by the
i. Imminent injury.
Tree in the last storm.

*The tree clutches sky
with cragged branches bent against
the depthless blue as
if carrying its
weight. Golden leaves and apples
guarded by Atlas,
whose cursed shoulders bear
everything separate. Many
say the tree reaches
all places and planes,
roots intrenched in death while limbs
launch upward, living.
A conduit, through
which earth, sky, gone, present, feed one
another. Though there are those
that still would scrape prize
from its bark, rake as much as
the hands can pilfer.*

A quick glance to your
blindness can save you before
changing split paint on

an exit from a
highway. The truck's stretched bellow
pulls you back into

your lane, the mirror,
side, elongated, being
heard in its narrow

miss. These things are a
substance flushed by the need for
continuing nerve.

There're the debates,
always heard, that maybe it's
best to keep your eyes

low, and take life as
it slides and strikes cheap with your
sight cut, like a carriage

horse, blinders banded,
trotting trolley tracks in the
city. The ticket

sellers want you to
forget that the saxophone
player you hear in

the street is better
than the one you hear from the
balcony. Unfed.

# Spring

Deciphering the stars:
I prefer the country's
flag un-bleeding,
the red not
stripes on the barber's totem—
belief though to be bent into
the brain, all slights
with the face unturned.

This all happens in my mind last night:
An email says my concealed
carry license is in the mail, so
I walk past my
mailbox every morning
looking out for the future.

What I notice in the grass:
The gray chicken looks like
a stump that looks
like a gray chicken.

The name of animal tragedies:
Geese snap their heads
back at passing cars
like flapping cartoons,
honking threats as
if behind their own fenders.
A man slaps one down with
his clipboard when it bites
for his face, attempting to protect
its nest nearby in the Target
back lot, beak clacking
against dull composite.
Later, a goose pecks madly
at the bottom of a car door. I
don't know if it senses
something inside, or if
it aims to
murder its own reflection.

*The stately geese march
smartly through the smooth
stone of Odysseus' palace
as Penelope watches,
a small ember of joy
in her unthinkable patience.
They snap up wheat grains
from the troughs of water,
her eyes trailing the tremors
of their successive chews,
water flaking into
small light-catching gems.
Her synapses seek some
semblance of sense-making,
husband off in a
distant unknown
history, sounds of her
undesired suitors—their
chortles, quarrels, and song—
fracturing through the halls.
She observes the geese,
ivory showing at her lips,
a small crystal forming
at the bottom blade of her eye.
The geese dip into the troughs,
withdraw quaking with their
devouring, their regal beaks,
razors, circling her as
her unexpected protectors.*

Tomorrow I see yesterday:
The vote jumped
backwards years.

I randomly find a fossil:
Under a rock, an ancient shape.
Under another, a serpent.

*The stone is difficult to*
*dream in. Eyes don't*
*shut. Hope is that*
*the stars are darkened*
*by stratus, so consciousness*
*can rest. The soldier*
*often wishes for the past*
*possibility to blink*
*at the casting moment,*
*which other times he knows*
*would have left him*
*questioning whether he was*
*already floating through death.*
*His pupils remain*
*unadjusted, sight's frame locked*
*to where Medusa's eyes had*
*resided in air, now*
*replaced by a blurred green,*
*yellow to brown under blue,*
*sometimes gray, orange,*
*pinks and reds, the black*
*always inevitable, restless*
*when punctuated by starlight.*
*And in the eardrum, now*
*gripped from receiving and*
*relaying signal, final*
*memory is the sharp hiss issuing*
*from the choir of tangled snakes.*

When attempting:
Art exhausts definition,
or definitive value, is
an endless unending ceasing
of individual authority.

Thinking about the you:
This poetry should
be what is wanted.
This is my unrelenting fault.

When scrolled to a blank page:
I haven't written a word.

I just think about my nose:
And it bleeds.

# Summer

It's summer and I jump
slightly less high than
last year, my body
heavier when I address
a sphere through a hoop
in Ohio's humidity, a
fox crossing the church
lot for its burrow
clearly set amidst the
peripheral brush, my
knees more achy than
other turns I've turned
as I turn to observe its
fire-orange
gallop, my left shoulder
lowering from the angle
that still sears nerves
from the impact that left
wreckage along a North
Bend intersection, within
which I watched the deployed
airbag deflate through the
ruptured engine's sharp haze,
lifted my fiancé's face in
my hands, sheeted by
relief to see strands of hair
were not the red lacerations
they first appeared to be in
shadow, an exact week before
our wedding, its impossibly
perfect rainstorm afternoon.

We're in Paris, record highs
in warming, hunting for air
conditioning and attempting to
avoid public restrooms for
the gambler's roll that some
don't have toilet seats. This
is compounded by the perspiration
ever-present on my face and arms
and clothes. Though this
does not diminish the city
flowering around us,
arriving from time,
architecture shouldered
and jointed with sculptures,
streets hinged
on masterpieces, or cafés
like Le Pure,
a beer cold to the
layout open to the heat,
*frites* like gold karats in
the midday light's wash, their
snap between the teeth, or
Le Select, its
whiskey sour, seats green
and white, or La Closerie
des Lilas, its
daiquiri a translucent pink,
my wife smiling over a layered
Irish coffee, four roasted beans
petaled on top, the 1920's clad
bartenders working art into taste,
lush wood grain lit through
shelves of glass bottles, the
pianist arriving mid-drink to
unpack notes that
scoop air into ice cream,
half-populated buried gems we
walked past tourist-crammed
cafés to grasp. Later, Le

Cathédrale Notre-Dame, its
spire collapsed from the
fire two months before,
rises over the river in full
marvel like a magnificent brace,
its gargoyled towers carrying
the sky's dimension of cloud
and blue as we sit drinking an
iced café crème and a large
bottle IPA at a table
outside Shakespeare
and Company Café, where,
juxtaposed, we rove
famous shelves
while still trying to
starve heat
tides through paper
tunnels, old walls
rippled with bindings.
Condensation puddles
around a bottle's base.

A stone hand holds a rose
placed by a walking
memory, fresh and the
mind's flesh in color,
above a name surrounded
by names archiving out
in faceted layers like
artichokes of land,
architecture, heartbreak,
a heavily petaled grief,
sharp edges on coffins,
crosses, obelisks, spires,
no wonder they make
the section signs softer
shapes, the walls topped
with double-toothed
daggers, piercing iron. A
chiseled open book on one
two-person grave shapes pages
like a gown's slopes hanging
deeply alone across a
lightless closet frame.
The temperature is once
again frying eggs in my
imagination. I pull my
darkened hat down even
tighter, swipe it up, a
windshield-wiper utility,
my earthy sandals crunching
against rocks in the dry rows'
fluctuating altitude. Patches
of yellow grass and weeds
brush my ankles, painting
presence more
into my awareness, the
qualification of time, as
I pass days swarmed
by days, hyphens
winged by numbers

bracketing life.
Checking the maps
we snapped with our
phones, we comb Père
Lachaise Cemetery for
the markers struck
with known names. Jim
Morrison, grave
securitized by a sticker-
littered metal
gate many jump to place
flowers and photos and
tiny icons, peace signs
and fallen petals. Colette,
two flowers with crossed
stems resting on her
grave's smooth face.
Chopin. Delacroix's
gold letters on black.
Apollinaire, his marker
jagged, as if forged and
signed by lightning.
Proust. Gay Lussac.
The palindrome of Léon
Noel. And Oscar Wilde,
grave sadly framed
by plexiglass to protect
the stone, carved into
a flying soul, from
recurring vandals
attempting desecration
with plagued ideas.
I reach up over the glass
to touch the soul's hand.

Our last night in Paris
a line of ambulances
half-circle below
us and to our right
as we wait outside Museé de
L'Orangerie in dark
green park chairs
at dusk for the lighting
of the Eiffel Tower, its
brightening glow, less
than 24 hours before we
watch the U.S. and
France meet in the World
Cup, fans from both sides
shaking *good match* in
the Marriott bar after.
We left with the
morning, regretting
every Paris street we passed
without knowing its turn,
along the angled veins of the
Seine River, fences peppered
with personalized locks,
the contours of my wife's face
staring out at the open-air fruit
stand at the front of *un marché*
from the back of a taxi.

The fox I never saw
disintegrates into its
burrow, leaving
only its flame in
my imagination, my
wife's words as she
points, her eyebrows
steepled in awe, two
weeks after we pulled
our canoe from
the shallow Little
Miami River and stood
in the shade of a boat
shed until we turned
to see two empty
kayaks sliding by the
gradual embankment,
people in the cold river
swinging fists and their
paddles' blade-like profiles,
blood smothering water,
97 degrees under sky
and alcohol, numbers
slathering into a brawl,
ten people into
twenty in less than
comprehensible seconds.
Angry tattoos on weather-
reddened skin waltzed in
the fray until a police
cruiser ushered dust into
the adjacent dirt
clearing, the lone officer
footing rapidly toward
the bloodshed, taser
drawn, shouting fierce
imperatives into
the surprisingly dry air;
though in his look

was an apprehension,
a fear the taser's one
shot would force
him to gun.

I turn back to the basketball,
its ease of rotation. A week
from now one thousand three
hundred and twenty nine miles
to the south, a racist will enter
a Walmart with a high-powered
rifle, and thirteen hours later,
forty six miles to my north,
an uncompromisingly completely
legal semi-automatic with
hundred round drum magazines
breaks open a street at 2 a.m..
I turn back to the
basketball and to my wife,
the fox in the lot not forgotten.

*The Teumessian Fox cuffs the country-
side with its punishing jaws. The threat
keeps the Thebans imprisoned in their homes
or risking massacre even simply at market.
Gargantuan paw prints press into blood-
soaked soil, a dark odor emanating
from teeth patrolling the walls of
the city. The fox is far too large and
fast to catch, delivered by the gods to be
forever unsolvable. The city becomes
strangled by impossibility. The air of
decay and orange fur permeates the populous,
until an Athenian shows with Lailaps,
the giant hound from whom nothing
escapes, to challenge inevitability.
The paradox is brought to a proper boil,
a vortex of closing range, distance
dividing by half each second, a
gaining without gaining,
until thrown into stone by Zeus,
a great action into great stillness,
imminent death against its obvious solution,
perpetuity statued.*

# Late Summer

Impossible hypotheses
are a real current pounding
through our daily movement,
cutting paths in rock
with belief and its
dissolution. Every
day is an unnoticed epic.
The untethered heat, the
balcony wood weathered
into a ship's hull. I scroll
through news and statistics
expectantly, numbers saying
somewhere in Cincinnati a
doctor's pen spells fentanyl.
The American scale does
not expect the person with
whitened teeth dying
from an aggravated back
injury prescription
used to treat opiate
dependency, pushed
by defendants in the
case that banned those
same defendants down
the avenue of an antidote
to their own poison,
and they make even
more coin staving their
profitable epidemic.
The cure is sold
by the cause. And
the person labeled addict
is blame's sad transaction,
gavel on skull,
when it's hair strand across
razor, and less than powder
on a penny can kill. I flip
the meatloaf in my microwavable
meal, think about the gym later.

The heat, untethered, like
California, or a needle. I
close the glass door. Through
it the air looks clean over the trees.

\*\*\*\*\*\*\*\*\*\*

On the opposite way of the 275
a parabolic trove of headlights
ignites rain into diamond
reminders of lives, a parade
of autonomy often thought
robotic. Windshields, dark
and reflective, water gilding
them silver, are all
slightly recognizable actors
role-playing the same movie
seen over again. They either
have gazes or are buried behind
anonymity's evil convenience,
helmet and visor.
It is more simple when the eyes
can't be looked into. Empathy
resides in the retinas, how the
pupils flex in shade. Lids
split wide, masked
by precedence, don't result
in seeing the horror before they
are strung from a paradigm.
Numbers without names.
After the rain, we walk through
humidity we wear on our
foreheads, stepping aside for cars on
the Ohio streets with no sidewalks.
The Western Hills drop to a forest
horizon behind us, numbing
the knowledge of the metal and
mortar maze zagging between its
roots. The wet air shallows my
breath. Another hurricane off
the coast converts to a Category 5.

The cicadas' high buzz throbs
from the backdrop off 4th and
Gaulbert in Louisville,
Kentucky, the hot early
September air clear between
brick apartments and the
tavern on the corner, most
everyone wearing red on
red, feathered logos, most
everyone able to speak
football, the rookie safety,
the quarterback's eye
doctor's days off, the name
of the punter's father's
barber, all alight with the
possibility of an unplayed
season, blue gold and green
Notre Dame drops moving
amongst the local insignia,
subcultures attempting
to temper competition's
slope, how it can slide into
violence. Churchill Downs,
mint juleps, the tall angles
of Cardinal Stadium, lots
so vast and packed they
shimmer with collective
motion, all dominoed
for sport, for the vested
belief, and the beautiful
lack of vested control.
On the field, players
orchestrate volume
from the layered crowd,
wound like a bloomed
rose, with their
gladiatorial sacrifice as
conductor. A macrocosm
of gathering, and I see a

stadium policeman with his
hand bracketing his mouth,
jaw jerking rapidly, pacing
toward one of the tunnels.
My thoughts panorama the
grandiose arena, and
sink to the invisible channels
skating between realities.
I watch with new awareness,
the officer dodging cheerleaders
and alumni until, almost to
the tunnel, he draws his hand
away, holding a shiny stick
of red licorice, not a radio,
no pulled weapon in the crowd,
as the band still thunders with
a long hopeless fourth quarter
bravado. I turn back to the game.
Even the known blimp, above
the stadium's razor,
with light dried from the sky,
takes on the paralyzing
presence of a shark just below
the inverse of its wheelhouse,
patiently awaiting reminding.
The cicadas' song, in its
constancy, is accepted by
the ears, unseen
though always there.

*Tithonus' mind creases
into itself, folding, facet
upon facet, too many
years to dream into.
Gifted immortality,
though not
agelessness, his
mouth shapes sounds
unrelated to language,
eyes barely able to discern
the anchor of time's
brilliant dawn, Eos, the
only image his thoughts
can still decipher, his
love the only clarity
in a wild violence
of pathos. Her eyes eclipse
in a dimming wind,
her hand through his
blotted hair a slowing
to his strobing awareness.
He has spun in this
shambled existence too
long, she decides, feeling
the reeling of fragmented
sanity within him. She
releases all save two fingers
from his head, two places
from where grow long lashing
antennae. His eyes swell red,
his mouth shrinks, he feels
a yellow fluttering birthing from
his shoulder blades, his limbs
stretching long and thin. With
this metamorphosis arrives
a vast hush in his
consciousness; cold
clearing focus. He looks
up from his lowering*

*orientation, his arrayed vision
searching for the goddess no
longer present. His wings
pulse in panic, and he clings
to the branch of a nearby
olive tree. With a renewed mind
there is now a sweeping loss,
the stab of her absence
for what he knows
is eternity. This
takes hold his insect
skeleton, and his abdomen
begins to quake in anguish,
shattering the air with requiem.*

# Early Fall

It's mid-nineties
in degrees
mid-September,
when all of the fall
monopolies color
their labels, umber
and amber embers
seasoning the city's
green. Debate
stages amass more
desperation. Pools for
communities shut.
The sweat that marbles
the abridged walk to
my Nissan reminds that
some seasons whisper,
others grow verbose.
Descending leaves trail
shadows across the
onramp, and for a moment
I fear killing
lizards I imagine
are chasing this late
throw of summer.

Watching Bob Ross on Netflix,
I think, trees have it easy, content
on water and earth to exist,
simple, as a praying
mantis bleached from molting,
bathing in the bullion of
a streetlamp in an employee
parking lot minutes after a California
10pm, in an aisle's exact middle,
halting, if for a shortened moment,
a conversation with a coworker, as
I lower myself to admire its assuming
pose, simple in the night's silence,
as an artichoke, its heart carved into
a bowl, with olive oil and feta, from
the barbed scales that mask it.

*From their initial encounter,
Cynara feels Zeus' eyes
slowly swallowing.
Zeus, visiting his brother,
Poseidon, discovers
a stirring he never expected.
Married to Hera, he hesitates
for an all too human time,
befallen by the thinnest skin
around Cynara's eyes, blushed
purple, her dress a perfectly
warped bell, silk to which
he sews his sight. He
makes her lips eclipsed
moons, her hair into asteroid
rings around a planet, and asks
her which things she wants
him to name her name. He
potteries her into a goddess,
hands gentle against her
spinning frame. Though Cynara
desires home more than him,
the father of gods, and subtly slips
away to ease her displacement.
Zeus sees this flight, her absence
a wounding lapse in his power,
and his anger scours,
plants her into the ground, dark
green walls, edged with teeth, rising
around her. She sinks, screaming
as they close over her, sealing
her at the center, beauty now
supplanted by deceiving leaves.*

# Crown

A man I haven't seen
in 24 years stands
on my Ohio balcony.
On some subconscious
level I know
this is my subconscious,
coal black hair I've never
seen as grayed as it is now,
a cigar turning between
fingertips, the lit end
doubling the low orange moon.
A Cohiba he passes to me
as I step through the open glass.
The smoke twines.

The smoke twines
as I step next to
something a son may take
as ordinary. I take
in the age in his face, the
differences missing from
memory, weathered flesh
at the eyes, the surrendering
hairline. He looks out at the
landscape, the treetops
retreating into night's darkness.
I want to tell him about all the songs
he used to play when he was alive
that now I finally understand.

That now I finally understand,
he smiles, and I want to ask him
how he sees this ruptured modern
world through the synapses of
his history-craving brain. Though
I at first only tell him that I know
why he wanted me to try onions on
a cheesesteak in Philadelphia when
I was just a child, and that now I
eat onions on cheesesteaks, and that
time in the Target when I couldn't
find him, and he emerged from the red
aisles after the storewide intercom call,
I still almost cry at the recollection.

I still almost cry at the recollection
of his swiveling chin, worry pulling
at his face with insane weight,
the relief that then buoyed us both
as I stood waving next to an employee in
a red vest, which now recalls the
red knight from Medieval Times restaurant,
reaching for a morning star while we ate
game hen and gruel and drank tall
iced goblets of Pepsi, wearing our cardboard
crowns with royal flair. His glasses before
eye surgery, the way his hair tufted from the
back mesh of a baseball cap, memories that
earthquakes jog.

Earthquakes jog
a collective memory:
how not even ground
is reliable. Like a new
car that dials the wrong
voice-activated name,
now a missed call
doomed to be zombie.
And there, the ring
back. Those gnarled
surfacing fingers. That
joint knowing,
texting the rescuing
question, juke.

Question, juke,
is how it goes at every hearing,
I tell him. Adults flunking
decency. An old thing, he says,
darkness in plain light,
the accepted absence of obvious logic.
The country is cut, I say,
things are unfathomable—the border,
the cages and raids, denied
asylum, camps and starvation,
the refugees, the separated, the shot,
the ill gone overtly ignored and
statistically removed by politicians
with no math on their fact sheets.

With no math on their fact sheets,
they mime at podiums with empty
syntax. He says, this is
how the script always pages. And
I ask him to which words I should
set fire. Just talk, he says, and
the words will strike their own matches.
I hand the Cohiba back to him,
exhaling heavily the smoke,
breathing late September. I remember
the summer, before I told time,
that he brought home a duo of desert
tortoises that roamed our Valencia backyard,
mountains across the sky.

*Mountains across the sky,
Chelone, a nymph, standing
atop Khelydorea, watches as
the dusking sun makes them
seem to move, which never
misses its mark upon her heart.
And in twilight, she anticipates
the morning, when she anticipates
its end. Every chapter begins as
stirring as the last chapter's finale.
And she loves these moments, their threshold
to all the phenomenon of the elusive non-
pursuit of elusion, someone else's construction.
She lives in her own heaven.*

*She lives in her own heaven,
so when messengers call her
for Zeus' wedding to Hera,
she states she
will stay where
she sleeps, where she
sits and sees
the steeps and the stars
all reflect into one. And the
many messengers take back
her statement. And Zeus
sends Hermes in return. And
Hermes casts her and her
home into a river*

*Home into a river,*
*Chelone looks hurriedly*
*around for its face, its*
*floor, the hearth,*
*feels it grabbing*
*her spine, the weight,*
*its mortar, attaching*
*to her back, even*
*fabric hardening*
*into shell. Her home*
*now forever her burden,*
*as she drags herself from*
*the water with her shortened*
*four limbs.*

Four limbs
pulled each shell
across our backyard's
Southern California dirt,
the sky an
aged photo gold,
outside the first house
I remember moving
from, playing with Army
Ants, orange plastic
molded in military attire,
on the lawn as my parents
filled the brown Mazda,
carrying boxes of our past.

Carrying boxes of our past,
I step back into the moment
with my father, staring at
fireflies flashing low
to the flora beneath us. Now
I want to hand him the
things he has missed, degrees
of accomplishment, birthdays,
and beers that a father and son
on so many occasions should have
shared. Packing a car with
every possession. Seeing Salt Lake's
violet ranges, the Nebraskan insect
clouds around gas station lights.
How his sons reunited in Ohio.

How his sons reunited in Ohio,
under a massive midnight sky,
the pain and fortune of sharing
their history. I tell my dad
about my brother and his
family, his love for his children
that reminds me of his. About
moments experienced etched
eternally in emotional
memory. About how,
on the drive home after
holding my niece on the day
she was born, I was suddenly
aware of the orbit of all things.

Aware of the orbit of all things,
perspective rains into the brain,
I say, and my
wedding, it made so many
things into what they should be.
Your name was there, I say,
I just wish you could have been.
I was, he says. He passes
the Cohiba once again to me.
And my wife, I wish
you could have met my wife, even
just once, you would love her, I say.
I already do, he says.
A man I haven't seen.

# Fall

Asleep's fall wakes me.
This isn't autumn.
The skyline builds into view.
Climate mirages the 71.
This is the curve of a lens.
The material between moments.
You're negotiating a home
purchase, looking
out the fragile glass of a
hospital at its own massive angles,
red brick that would be almost
aesthetic without the reminder
of the current current, that time
is a tangible you can't quite hold,
sitting in an ICU room, brimming.

Winter wheels around again,
impeachment on
political lips, crucial
fruit for the starving.

I have always been hurtling
toward where I am now,
and where I am now is
family. Give life
to me wherever I am not,
whenever I am not, for
my home is forever on this line.

**Jacob Minasian** received his MFA from Saint Mary's College of California, where he was the 2016 Academy of American Poets University and College Poetry Prize winner. He is the author of the chapbook, *American Lit* (Finishing Line Press), and his work has appeared in publications including *Poets.org, The Museum of Americana, RipRap Literary Journal, Cathexis Northwest Press, CP Quarterly, Windows Facing Windows Review, Sledgehammer Lit,* and *Fire and Rain: Ecopoetry of California* by Scarlett Tanager Books, among others. Originally from California, he currently lives with his wife and daughter in Cincinnati, Ohio.

www.ingramcontent.com/pod-product-compliance
Lightning Source LLC
Chambersburg PA
CBHW030224170426
43194CB00007BA/854